CW01457153

Soulmates:

Not All Are in The Form of Lovers

MOONSOULCHILD

The Feelings & Healing Collection:

Finding Self: Journey to Self-Love
Healthy Connections: Guide on Relationships
Grief: Process of Healing

Broken: For the Ones Picking Up the Pieces
Discovering: For the Soul Searchers
Twin Souls: For the Lovers

Toxic Connections: Freeing Your Demons
Healing: The Journey of Growth
Soulmates: Not All Are in the Form of Lovers
Insecurities: Empowering Self

Soulmates

I have always believed in soulmates. At one time I believed we had one soulmate and the search for them was tough, but when we ended up finding them, it would be us forever. I was incredibly wrong, I still believe we do have soulmates, but now I see it in a different aspect. I believe we have many soulmates throughout our lifetime, and not all are in the form of lovers. I believe we meet people that spark a soul connection, something that's undeniable, something out of this world. I have met many in this lifetime, some around still around, and some have existed in some form. I believe friends can be soulmates. I believe family can be soulmates. I believe you shouldn't overlook a connection you have with someone, to always express those feelings and live through them. In this collection, I will give you my experiences with the many soulmates who have entered my life, and ones who left, and how it's important to know you don't need to keep them in your life just because you have a soul connection.

We have multiple soulmates in our lifetime, and
not all are in the form of lovers.

Get the illusion that every soulmate is a lover. It's a friend. It's family. **It's a connection that can't be repeated**, a unique feeling that can only be felt within that soulful moment. The catch, you will meet many, and *all will be a different feel.*

A soulmate isn't everyone you love throughout your life. A soulmate is someone who walks into your life and teaches you a love you never felt. It's a connection your heart can't deny. An unbreakable force. Not just a lover, a soulmate can come in all forms, **cherish them all**.

When we're young, we believe our soulmate is one person and one person only, but once you grow and connect with different souls, you will know who is a soulmate connection. A soulmate is someone who comes into your life and makes you feel something you've never witnessed; they will open your eyes to a side of yourself you never knew existed. They make their way to not only your heart but your soul. They teach you something. Sometimes soulmates come in and stay, and some come and go. They plant their seed, show their purpose, and either watch you grow or grow with you.

Soulmates come in all forms, lovers, friends, and family. I like to say, an undeniable connection. When your soul matches with your mate, it's something magical. I've met a lot of soulmates, some are still here with me, some are in heaven, and some are still out there in the world waiting for the right moment. I have loved and detached from some, but I still love them, and that love doesn't go anywhere. The lessons they taught me led me to my greatest purpose than anyone who I chose that was wrong for me, ones who taught me nothing.

A soulmate will always teach you, whether they stay or not, there's always a purpose. The hardest part for me was to understand they don't always stick around. To cherish the time they brought to me, remember the good, and remember why they left that mark.

Soulmates aren't just lovers, so please, stop fantasizing about that. Soulmates are souls that come into your life and touch your soul in ways not everyone can. **They made you feel something**. They teach you something. Even after their exit in your life, you still hold that love.

What do you believe a soulmate is?

Someone who will *know all*
my problems try to help.

Some *is I*

Someone *who try*

You keep I

to understand

We spend our lives searching for our soulmates,
just to find out *some aren't meant to stay*.

You'll know when you meet a soulmate, you'll be introduced to a part of yourself you never knew existed. They're around to open your eyes, and to love you, and some may bring you pain. **The forever scars**. They're special, they open your soul. *They're the reason you'll love yourself a little more*.

A soul who creates a connection of the vibration of each other. **A soulmate is someone who teaches you love and heartbreak**. They don't remain in your life forever, but you will always remember why they once were.

A letter to a soulmate:

Writing this letter to you is a release, but painful at the same time. Remembering everything that went down and trying to keep myself levelheaded. It's been almost 4 years since we went our separate ways, and that's because I decided to ghost you. Some people will say I didn't ghost you since I gave you many chances to understand and to see me in clarity, but you never did. You always chose to see me through the picture you painted, as the shy girl, the girl who only needed you. Once I started growing and being open with my wants in life, we started to grow apart. I never wanted to lose you, which is the reason I always tried to make it work. You were my best friend, but as we grew into our adult life and I saw the secret shade you threw my way, I realized there were things I was unable to share with you, so in that aspect, I blame myself for pulling away. You were very judgmental when it came to my life decisions and the things that made me happy, even if you spoke you supported me, your actions always proved you lied. After all these years I still can't understand why being my friend was so hard for you, because of the things I chose to explore in life. Is it because I didn't have enough time for you? Is it because I didn't dedicate all my time to you and your needs? Is it because I was no longer that shy girl, you felt you made? After all this time, I still don't understand why my best friend of so long couldn't accept who I was when I presented my true self. To you, I was always a copy. To you, I was never special or unique. To you, I was "your little sister" the annoying one, I remember those exact words. I always wondered if you would ever get off that high horse you put yourself on, to see how pathic you looked every time you chose to put me down, someone you claimed to love. I never wanted to be you, especially for that reason. The decisions you always made, the situations you always found yourself in, I didn't want any of that. What I did, was support you through all of them, as a friend would. I regret not being honest at the times you needed to hear "you shouldn't do that" instead, I remained quiet, mainly because my advice wouldn't be accepted. Our friendship was something I held onto for so long because you helped me open up and become the woman I am today. All your bad decisions, I learned not to repeat. All the friends you chose to pick, I chose to not be around. This letter may sound like there was never love there, but the love we shared is only felt by us both, and to this day, I remain with that love, I'm happy to do it from afar.

Soulmates: Not All Are in The Form of Lovers

Write a letter to a soulmate:

_____
_____
_____
_____
_____
_____
_____
_____
_____
_____
_____
_____
_____
_____
_____
_____
_____

Heavy on the **"If I love you, I always will"** so
when it ends, platonic or lover, *it always hurts
like hell.*

I realized it didn't matter how strong I was,
whether I was whole, letting go of someone I
loved always hurt. I'm a lover, so I don't ever
wish to lose love. I don't put myself in the
position to lose it. I never see it coming.
Knowing we outgrow, doesn't make it hurt less.

Even after someone has left my life, the love
remains. The memories stain. The moments are
so vivid in my heart. I never let go of the love, I
let the love take a new path. Letting the soul go,
while cherishing the time and the love that was
once felt. There's love in letting go.

Have you ever met someone to who you felt comfortable confessing your secrets? **Someone, you just feel safe with your heart**? no secrets, just vibes? *It's real.*

There are souls out there you'll meet and feel the instant connection, nothing more than that. At that moment, you're opening yourself without fear, making yourself completely vulnerable to every experience you've endured.

It's real, *it comes without force*. Soulmates, many of them come into your life and make you feel, they make you open yourself in a way you've never witnessed before. They come to love you, to teach you, to open yourself to find every version of you within every part of your growth.

They come in all forms, not just lovers. You can have many, not just one. A soulmate is more than someone you believe will share the rest of your life with because it's true, *soulmates may also leave you*.

They're around for the moment, however long it may be. Let go of any attachments you hold to find the perfect soulmate and try to make everyone you come across the one. Some will test, teach, read, open, and love you. Some may let you go or be forced to outgrow you.

The most important thing to remember, *love them and embrace every part of their soul at that moment*. Everything can't be predicted. Live in the moment, love at the moment. It's not the way to live, **it's the only way to feel alive**.

A letter to a soulmate:

Sometimes I don't know who to thank for your existence or even your presence in my life. I swear you're an angel sent from above, or the universe had you in my path for a while, but I wasn't ready for you. Even though you are who I've been searching for my whole life in human form. Except I, was always chasing the idea of you. I was chasing the idea of the perfect love. I was chasing the idea of how I should be loved. When I met you, times weren't perfect, our story wasn't a fairytale, it was a complete mess on my part. I was in a relationship, one I had been in for almost 4 years, one I didn't know I outgrew. You were kind and caring, and let me be open with you. I felt a force to you, one I couldn't let pass me, so, if that made me wrong, I take the accountability for ruining a heart. Once the events unraveled, the more I saw clearly, and I wasn't only to blame, it was just the times of deceit not on my part passed me. at that moment, every bad moment of my life came clear to me, I couldn't overlook it. I remember feeling confused, while crying my eyes out in my car parked somewhere, on facetime with you. You listened. You didn't mislead me, you always guided me while letting me make my own decision. You opened my eyes to my worth

I never realized. While I always came last, I finally put myself first. The memory that sticks with me the most, is deciding to come to visit you, to see if what we had was more than a friendship. Not only my heart, but my soul had this undeniable force, I needed to know.

You have been a powerful force. You have been such a light in my life. You have opened my eyes to so much I couldn't see in myself. The part that always gets me, is you never asked me to change a thing about myself, you loved me for who I am and that's what makes me so happy to be with you. I have never felt unconditional love until I've been loved by you. The way we support each other through our passions, the way we show our affection. I adore everything about you, there's nothing I would change. The way we met, the decisions we both made to be together, we just knew. Our hearts were meant to align. Our souls were meant to be one. When we're together, there's no fear, there's nothing that holds us back from being who we are. What we give to each other, is something no one can understand but us. So, if you ask me if this was worth it, I'd do it all over again with no regrets. Loving you, and being loved by you, has been a blessing and a miracle all in one. There isn't a soul out there who can compare, because yours is the one that fits me perfectly, I wouldn't ever give that away.

You gave me the most special gift of all, your love. *Pure, honest, unconditional love.* Thank you for loving me the way I've always loved. Thank you for showing me that it's possible to love even after you've lost all hope. **That real love and soulmates truly do exist**.

The "honeymoon" phase will never fade. Our love is intense, and real, and I'll never get tired of the affection, attention, or time you give me. your love is the only love I want every day for the rest of my life. I've never dreamt of a future with anyone as I dream of ours.

I went through many "wrong ones" to be prepared for your love. I had to grow as a woman to be prepared to give you the love you deserved, hurting you wasn't in the cards. I grew into the woman I am, ready to give the love I've prayed to receive.

I loved myself, then I loved you.

Falling in love with you was the best thing to ever happen to me, I never saw it coming, **that's what makes our love incredibly beautiful**. Our love is the kind people hope to find one day, the love I've prayed to find. That's how I know I deserve this love.

God gave me you.

Communication will take you to great lengths.
It will keep you in healthy connections. Don't
forget to be open, and honest, and
communicate how you feel. Let others know
how you feel for them too. No one deserves to
be in the dark when your heart isn't the only
one involved.

Be open.

Be transparent.

Communicate always, it's important to speak and express how you're feeling, without leaving anyone in the dark. It saves a lot of confusion and lost time. It saves closure you feel you never get.

Don't ever make anyone wonder why.

Be honest.

Be there.

Good connections always come to an end because communication is the hardest for people to do. I'd rather be hurt because of the truth than hurt being in the dark, wondering if it was me, or something I did. It's not okay to make anyone feel like they're not worth an explanation.

I believe in divine timing, *that everything happens at the exact moment it's meant to.* I believe we meet souls who fit into our lives at that exact moment. Whether it's to love us, help us, guide us, or teach us. I believe we meet many soulmates in our lifetime and not all are in the form of lovers, they come in all aspects of love, through connections. I believe we connect with many souls at what may be random moments to us, but to the universe, it's divine timing. I believe in the universe. I believe it brings me to every eye-opening experience, to every painful heartache. I believe it brings me to it, to make me strong enough to get through it. I've overlooked the signs the universe presented in my past because I wanted to live life at my standards, as I cried for forgiveness every time I sinned. I kept praying for love and to be whole, while I was searching for it within someone who couldn't provide what I needed to feel complete. I could only give that feeling to myself. I looked the other way when I replayed the many storylines and the universe told me to turn the page, I fought for it to make sense. My life has been about searching for the feeling of being whole and feeling loved. I was selfish and gave everything I could to everyone I loved, breaking myself into many pieces and trying to keep them whole. Those pieces are gone with their existence from my heart. I was taught a lesson from all the souls I fought to keep, or foolishly walked away from. I was taught to be strong, not everyone is meant to stay forever. I was taught to be mindful, not everyone will understand to accept all of you. I was taught to have an open heart, not everyone would love me the way I could love. I was taught to not analyze why it didn't work in my favor but to accept it worked in the favor the universe planned for me. I was taught to be patient. I was taught to speak it into existence, to shut out the negativity. I bloomed. I grew. I'm forever soul-searching. They're many soulmates I'll come across. They're many parts of me I haven't unlocked yet. I'm so ready to meet them. I live in the moment. I love it at the moment. To cherish every moment, I.

Souls come into your life at the moment you need them. **To teach you**, to *test you*, to love you. They're many reasons they enter. The saddest part of all, sometimes you never know the reason until they leave you.

A letter to a soulmate:

I'd start by saying our relationship wasn't all bad, especially in the beginning, it felt good. Even though we started wrong, under the circumstances. I should have never tried to save you from the demons of your past, or yourself countless times during our time together. I never blamed your lack of motivation to find your passion, nor did I blame your mental illness when times got dark. It was, just time for me to move on from you once our mental spaces collided and we weren't on the same page. I'm open with my emotions, even though I like a moment of alone time to get my thoughts in order, to not react off impulse and harsh words that will forever scar me. You hid when times got dark and never chose to communicate even after the light showed. You stayed within the shell you placed yourself in and never grew. You may blame it on your past, but your past was far past you, it was me, in your present, but you always overlooked me too. You were living in your past still, in hopes you would be cured of the heartache you endured all those years behind you. You loved me, I always believed that, but you didn't have what it took to love my whole being because you still loved what you left behind, or more so, what outgrew you. You couldn't let go of the pain, the burdens, and the love you once felt. Being with me was fun for you, someone who loved you unconditionally, something you said you never felt. I always felt special, to be able to give you exactly what you never had. Yet I was struggling to get the same love reciprocated because all I knew was the toxic love you were accustomed to. I never blamed you for the pain you brought to me, I blame myself for trying to heal a soul I had no business mending, knowing there was no certainty it would even happen. We made many great memories. We had many laughs and I'm grateful for all the happiness you brought to me at times I needed it. I'm thankful for the support you brought when you could, whether it was material or physical. It just was never there when it came to my emotional being, I needed more. It hurt seeing you in pain when I chose to walk away because at that moment I knew you loved me, but you didn't know what it's like to love all of me, at full capacity. I hid a lot of who I was to make you feel comfortable. I dimmed my passions to let you have your moments. I let go of people I loved, to be in your presence. I know now, that's not what love is. That's codependency. I loved you as much as I could, to the depths I knew I could, to try and keep you happy, through all the spirals of our moments together. I held the weight when it came to the scars. I held the weight when it came to recovering every heartache after every misunderstanding. I don't wish for the things I did at that time. Like for you to see me as a whole, to understand I'm more than who you saw me to be, only for your need. There were times you used me, but I let you. There were times you watched me slowly break, without trying to mend me. Times when communication could have saved many dark times, but you chose to blur me out, to the point you became blind. You thought I'd be right by your side forever, except the forever you believed wasn't long enough. You blame me, for breaking your heart and walking away from you. You blame me for the outcome of what became of us because you only saw my sins. You blame me for it all, never once took accountability for one moment that passed us. Playing the blame game won't change what happened or change the outcome of the growth that passed you but found me. I chose myself in the end. I chose to evolve, something I couldn't do being by your side. You took too much of me, I didn't have it left to save you any longer. I thank you, for the moments, the good and bad. If it wasn't for you, I wouldn't be this free. The way you secluded me, sometimes belittled me, broke me out of my shell. You brought me one of the great lessons, to always feel, soul-deep. So, I thank you. I thank you for always loving me in half, while I loved you in whole, it helped me understand the importance of loving myself more, which is why I ended up loving you less. I'm not sorry, so please, let it go.

If souls disappear from your life, don't chase them, and try to save what you thought you had. They chose the direction and path that doesn't involve you. Their heart's set, nothing you can do to change that. **Don't create heartache where love is never meant to live**.

The biggest lesson we all needed to learn the hard way, was chasing someone when they decide to leave our lives. We put so much pressure on *"what could have been"* we forget what truly was. We forget to look at the whole story, we are forced onto the chapter we haven't gotten to, or ever will. When someone decided to go, it may result in them ghosting you. Don't look for closure, or answers, there's nothing left to find because there was nothing in the first place. The more you fight for what you believe, the harder it will be once you try and keep them close. No matter what, you'll end up hurt. You'll end up wishing you could forget it all. Do yourself a favor, don't question the universe when it decides to take a soul out without reason, there's always a higher purpose, don't forget that.

Write a letter to a soulmate:

_____

_____

_____

_____

_____

_____

_____

_____

_____

_____

_____

_____

_____

_____

_____

_____

Once upon a time, **we all feel for someone who wasn't meant for that moment** or meant for us at all, but that didn't stop us. Once upon a time, we all fell for someone who wasn't healthy for our hearts, but *that didn't stop us from loving them.*

We all fell for someone who opened a part of our soul we couldn't overlook. Someone good at acting, while you gave your authentic self. Someone we weren't healthy for our heart, who didn't reciprocate everything. What they had to offer wasn't close to what you gave.

Someone who wasn't meant to be in that moment, or any moment, that didn't stop us from trying to hold them close. *Someone who brought us this feeling we didn't want to be without*. Someone who brought us this purpose we longed for, and the moment they left, that purpose left with them.

If something isn't meant for us, why do they cross our path? **Why make us involved just to break us apart**? Why make us question our worth? Why does it make us cold? why do we change our love language to be compatible with someone who is not meant to feel us, just because we feel them?

The power of the heart is endless, the love we're able to feel and receive amazes me. To love after hurting. To love after understanding the consequences. To love after knowing our love isn't reciprocated. *The power of how much our hearts can love, makes me feel superhuman.*

Soulmates: Not All Are in The Form of Lovers

I never gave up on love for that reason, if I wasn't meant to feel, I wouldn't behold this place for my heart to beat, feel, and love. I may have chased, searched, created, and prayed. I may have overstayed my welcome and overextended a connection that already outgrew me.

I'm not good with change, once I love you, I don't want to ever watch you go. Once I found something in you that makes me feel something that doesn't only open my heart but awakens my soul. Something that can't be compared, that I never felt or found anywhere, I refuse to go.

It's been a battle to let go of things I've become captivated by; I've become adapted to. That's where I always went wrong, holding everyone who felt different to a higher standard didn't make them feel the same.

Trying to make someone who was only meant to be temporary, a permanent place in my heart. it was like all the truth I knew went out the window, I was always blind when it was time to let go.

A message to a soulmate:

When I think of you, I think of my vulnerable self. I think of the times when I was so desperately in need to be loved. When I think of you, I think of how my heart almost broke trying to make you love me, even after you massacred every piece. I was infatuated with you, completely love drunk off the idea of who you could be. Completely high off the thought of what we could be, because of the fantasy you brought to me. You were so good with words, words that were so beautifully spoken, except for one problem, no action to ever prove, and there I was, a fool. I loved you very much, so much I waited for you. We lived miles apart, maybe that's why my drive was always to fight harder for you. Even after you were exposed, and I saw a piece of the real you, I stayed true, I didn't stop loving you. I was infatuated with this fantasy you convinced me to believe, the one you spoke so beautifully. There I was, a beautiful fool, blinded by this pathic dream of you loving me. When we finally met, years later and decided to give us a try, after the cards we'd drawn many times proved this wasn't destined for us, I needed to give it everything. I took so much of myself to love you, and I can't blame you for that. I can't blame you for the pain brought to me after your real self showed within the shadows of love I created for you. I can't blame you because I kept you around even after your manipulating ways. You were so good at lying. You were so good at making me believe you loved me too. I think the part that always gets me, is knowing you never showed aggression towards me, you never belittled me, and you always showed passion. You supported my dreams and showed me what a true friend is, and for that I thank you. I thank you for never speaking words of regret, making me forever hold without closure. It's just, you chose to break my heart in other ways. You chose to play with my heart, while you lived two different lives. One with me, and one with her. You cheated on me the whole time, as I should have known. Your infidelity wasn't new to me, so I guess I can't blame you for that. After all these years, when I think of you, I try to understand how someone can be so misleading. I try to understand how someone can be so cold, to let someone love them so much without being honest with the fact you never loved me too, and if you did, you didn't deserve it. You came back to tell me how sorry you were, to have brought the kind of pain you did. Your apology isn't something I wanted or needed, I couldn't believe a damn thing you ever said to me, why would I now? The closure wasn't anything I needed from you, I got that for myself by healing from your presence in my life. Back then, I swore I wasted so much time. I thought I wasted moments I could have been loved by someone else. I thought about the moments I could have erased your memory and somehow your existence from my life altogether. I prayed to forget you. I was 16 when we first met, and I was 19 when I chose to let you go. Sometimes I question why I loved you. Sometimes I question why I gave you a chance. I was young, lost, and vulnerable. If I had to blame you for anything, it would be taking advantage of my heart knowing you weren't going to love me as I deserved to. I didn't deserve to be led on, lied to, and lost. I didn't deserve to grieve you when you disappeared. I didn't deserve to wonder what you were doing when you were ghosting me. I didn't deserve to be the second soul in your life, the one who was hidden while you lived your double life. I didn't know what I deserved, which is why I held onto you for so long, hoping it was you. Turns out, you never deserved me. When someone asks me who was it, the one who hurt me the most. It's you, it's always you. Even though we weren't together for years, and you didn't abuse me in any form, it's still you. You had the power in your being to break me and you chose to let that happen. I always thought it would hurt more to be with someone for so long, than the need to live without them. It wasn't, it was a fantasy I created the love I never got to feel back, and how I created my heartbreak.

Have many soulmates do you think you've met throughout your life?

_____

_____

_____

_____

_____

_____

_____

_____

_____

_____

_____

_____

_____

_____

_____

_____

A letter to a soulmate:

When I think of you, the first thing that comes to my mind, is I miss you. I miss you so much. Next month will be 4 years since you turned into an angel, and I miss you in human form so much. Sometimes I wish I could text you, come visit you, and just enjoy the presence of each other. Sometimes I wish I could hear your voice. Sometimes I wish I could feel your touch. Sometimes, I just wish to feel you. I wish to hear how proud you are of me and to hear your feedback on every blessing that's made its way into my life after your departure. It breaks my heart how all my blessings appeared after I lost you, grieved you, and continue to heal from you. I never understood why I had to lose you to gain so much beauty in my life. It's like a part of me feels empty due to the lack of understanding when it comes to living without you. It was your constant signs that held me together, to keep going, and to strive harder. It was you, who lead me to become the woman I am today. The strong, fearless, and free spirit I am. I know you already know that I know our souls are connected because of those exact reasons, we were fiercely free and, in your presence, I could embrace all of me. I don't like to talk about my regrets or the things I wish I could have done, because I know it's not important. I don't wish to live with guilt because I know there's nothing I could have done differently; you knew your place in my life and how much I loved you. It was never guilt I felt, it was true heartbreak. It was the feeling of being numb, something I never thought I could feel being someone with a big heart. I remember the actual feeling of my heartbreak, the depression that awakened inside me and left me feeling alone. There wasn't anyone I could run to, I felt alone. Keeping your spirit alive, through the moon kept my sanity high. Today, I still search for you on the moon and every time, I feel you. Your presence, even after death, has been a powerful force. I never thought I could feel something so strong with you in spirit, I thought I lost everything when you passed. I can still remember the exact day, and the exact moment and feeling. Every time I rethink it, I feel it all over again. Except for today, I miss you, but I've made peace with the emptiness I'll always feel without you here. I made peace with the understanding you never left me, your soul and spirit are still guiding me. I truly am the most grateful for your presence in my life. You are someone who played the biggest part in helping me become the woman I am, with your friendship, I was able to let go of everything that wasn't for me, to accept the real blessings. My soul is so fiercely free, because of you. You will always be my favorite.

Soul connections are rare, but they're endless and special. Soul ties are forever embedded in the heart and memory.

It's something beautiful, meeting someone who is connected soulfully, not many can get that far when it comes to knowing you. They get to the heart and burden themselves there. My love has been too intense for some, some never got past my heart.

If I loved you, I loved you, but I didn't love you enough to be naked, bearing my whole soul to you. You may have brought comfort, but not protection. You didn't make me feel free, you caged me in. Many didn't understand my free soul, so they let me go. Many didn't understand my growth, they tried to stunt it and I left them behind. I loved them very much, they opened my heart and taught me how to love, how to care for another soul, and how to give.

They also taught me what love wasn't and what pain feels like, to feel broken. They taught me many emotions and how to heal. They taught me how to love, but not what it feels to be loved in return. They taught me how to give, but never receive. They taught me the more you show your authentic soul, the more you'll lose but the more you'll also gain with souls I connect with my free soul. I'm thankful for those souls.

If you've touched my soul, **you're rare**.
I don't even need to tell you,
You will know off my energy alone.

Everyone who walks into your life has a purpose, whether you know the reason. Everyone who makes you feel alive was aligned on your path on purpose. Everyone you meet has a will, a test, or a place in your heart. **The universe doesn't place any soul on your path by accident**.

I'm a firm believer you should never look the other way when presented with someone who brings you something you can't live without. *I'm a firm believer you don't meet any soul by accident*, they all have a purpose, and it doesn't matter if you understand the reason.

The hardest part for me is trying to not overthink "**why**" or trying to understand why I won't ever know. Did this soul enter my life for a test? I tend to overthink. I tend to try and find answers to things that don't need to be explained, only felt.

I've learned to embrace every moment, big and small. To live within every moment. To unlearn my impatient behavior. To unlearn my overthinking. To unlearn my obsession with wondering why.

I understand to be at peace in life is to be open to living in the moment. It takes a lot of patience and being free. It's changing, how I live currently and let the universe choose for me. once I trusted the universe to take what was not meant for me and replace it with what I needed, I haven't looked back since. I trust it. I believe the universe will always align with what I need at the exact moment. To be thankful is an understatement. Blessed is a better word. To have amazing souls enter my life and teach me something new about myself. To have amazing souls enter my life and make me feel something different. To meet amazing souls is a blessing to see how they tie into who I am.

Don't overlook anyone's place in your life, and don't try to find out why they were placed there. Thank the universe for its blessings **and fully live every moment possible**.

On my spiritual journey, **I found you**. *it was like looking into a mirror of my soul*. I was whole on my own for the first time, but I saw my reflection in you. you opened my eyes to a life outside the one I thought I wanted. **My soul felt at home** when I met my twin flame, you.

Don't stop searching for your soulmate. **Don't give up**. You'll go through a lot of countless disappointments to find them, but the search will be worth it. Once you let go of the bitterness of past loves and embrace the reciprocated love, you'll see it's worth it.

When you meet your soulmate, you'll feel it instantly. *A chemistry that will never go unnoticed* and a feeling you should never overlook.

There are souls I met that weren't meant for me in this lifetime, but *our connection is beyond the norm*, something uniquely placed in my life. I can't forget. I can't replace it. The only explanation possible, **I believe I may have met them in my past life**.

Soulmates: Not All Are in The Form of Lovers

There are souls I met that weren't meant for me in this lifetime. *They were uniquely placed in my life, I can't forget them.* Divine timing. I trust the universe to bring and take souls who've outlived their purpose and bring new ones through for reasons beyond my knowing. Some aren't for me, weren't meant for this lifetime, just a lesson. I've always been big on vibes because energy doesn't live. I've always been in touch with auras. When someone is more than a flame, who leaves their imprint, leaves a connection lasting in my memory, that's special. I've had many soulmates enter and exit my life, both out of my control. I loved them at the moment and lived out the story to the point it outgrew us. I'm thankful for the time. I think about it often, the souls I lost but couldn't keep, realizing they weren't a possession, they never belonged to me. I chased and tried badly to make the universe align our paths through our growth. I didn't realize time ran out. I didn't realize these souls who entered my life who sparked a deeper connection and rare moment, I'd one day need to let them go. Back then, I wouldn't have been okay, but now I'm grateful for those same souls leaving. Every good connection isn't meant to stay the same, I guess that's why it's rare, you feel something for the moment, and it feels like it's been forever.

I just feel the world has it so wrong when it comes to love and holding onto souls who no longer serve us purpose. The world has the wrong idea of love. You love, but not through unhealthy times. Sometimes you need to let go and trust the universe to align your path. If these same connections arise on your way, seek them, but don't hold onto anything that doesn't want to be kept.

Don't overthink why someone exists in your life, not everything is deeper than presented. Take it for what it is, if it's truly meant for you, if they're truly meant to align with you, you'll find them somewhere in your next chapter.

In your next lifetime.

Don't be afraid to explore the connections you have with people. Don't be afraid to love who the universe presents in your life at the exact moment they walk in. I believe we have many, don't overlook anyone who presents a soul connection, *your heart will know*.

Soul connections are so rare, *I cherish them*. Life is peaceful when you **choose people who choose you**, and who love you wholeheartedly. Keep those people around, the ones with a peaceful comfortable vibe, but also made it to your soul.

Fearless and fiercely in love with you. *You always bring out the best in me.* You've set me free in ways you never understood could help me love myself. With your guidance, support, and love, **I'm my greatest self**. With your soul, I can be comfortable in my skin without fear.

Thank you for giving my work a chance. I pray you chose to get this book to feel what I had to offer from my experience. It's a mix of many emotions and truths within my journey. It took me some time to withhold this information for it to stick. I hope you find peace within my words and understand what a true soulmate is and the lessons they bring. I hope you found that within reading. I hope you found the beauty in letting go. Come back to this book whenever you need reminders. **Highlight**. Write notes.

For more of my work:

Email: moonsoulchild@outlook.com
Instagram: @moonsoulchild
Twitter: @moonssoulchild
Facebook: @moonsoulchild
Tiktok: Bymoonsoulchild
Apple Music: Moonsoulchild
Spotify: Moonsoulchild

Printed in Great Britain
by Amazon